James Tumbridge is a barrister and an Intellectual Property Litigation partner at Venner Shipley, a European Intellectual Property firm. James has been a litigator for 20 years, and has extensive experience in commercial litigation, intellectual property and alternative dispute resolution. He has a uniquely international experience having worked and appeared in courts in the USA, Canada, the UK and British Overseas territories. He is the author of 'Tumbridge's Guide to Legal Qualification: The Common Law World', and a co-author of 'Drafting Patents for Litigation and Licensing'; and co-author of 'Privilege and Professional Confidences: An International Review'.

Ashley Roughton is a practicing barrister and has been in practice in technology based areas of law, principally Intellectual Property law and competition for over 25 years. He is also a teaching member of the department of Law at Queen Mary, University of London. Ashley is a co-author of the competition annex of the CIPA guide and also writes a number of chapters for both 'The Modern Law of Trade Marks' and 'The Modern Law of Patents' (of which he is chief editor).

A Practical Guide to the Ownership of Employee Inventions – From Entitlement to Compensation

A Practical Guide to the Ownership of Employee Inventions – From Entitlement to Compensation

James R. Tumbridge
Barrister of Lincolns Inn and the Middle Temple,
Partner of Venner Shipley

Ashley Roughton
Barrister of the Inner Temple, Barrister at Law
(Northern Ireland and the Republic of Ireland)

Law Brief Publishing

Published 2020 by Law Brief Publishing, an imprint of Law Brief Publishing Ltd
30 The Parks
Minehead
Somerset
TA24 8BT

www.lawbriefpublishing.com

Paperback: 978-1-913715-25-0

PREFACE

Employee entitlement, as it is often called, is an important aspect of patent law and yet is rarely seen in reported cases. Collaborations and accidental discoveries or inventions by employees can lead to significant changes in bargaining power and rights as between employees and their employers. In many cases a few simple precautions, dealt with at the beginning of a relationship, can save a great deal of trouble later on. This book will guide you on the key issues to understand and the immovables; first no employee, who is not employed to invent (though this expression has a special meaning), can be deprived of their invention without decent consideration and secondly (and even then) any employee, who is employed to invent, can be deprived of their invention but may have a right to substantial compensation in the right cases, though compensation is pegged to success so that a valueless patent will not result in anything but a negligible award of compensation.

The aim of this book is to provide a quick and simple guide to what the issues are and what sort of questions to expect from your lawyers in the event of a dispute (or if you want to forestall one). With the guidance we offer you should be able to assess your position with greater clarity and understand the issues common to the question of whether an invention was created by an employee and who owns any resultant patent.

In this book we have spent some time commenting on the Shanks case since it is the first time that a case on employee compensation for a patent has hit the big time, both in terms of the level of the award and also in terms of the seniority of the court finally entertaining the award. The result was surprisingly pro-employee.

We have endeavoured to state the law as at 1 October 2020.

James Tumbridge
Ashley Roughton
October 2020

CONTENTS

CHAPTER ONE
INTRODUCTION

1.1. Employee inventions are inventions created by someone who is an employee of another person or corporate entity, their relationship to their employer and the nature of their duties as an employee means that the right to apply for a patent to an invention created by the employee vests with the employer. However, there are many variables to determine whether the employment relationship is effective and operates to vest those rights in the employer. This book will explain the relationships and how rights operate. Employment relationships might seem straight forward, but problems can arise; especially if the employee has more than one employment relationship, is engaged in a peculiar way and their employment terms are unclear. Further issues in consequence of unique factual circumstances, such as if the employment is part time or short term, or if it is unclear who devised which parts of an invention and when, so that you cannot be clear if they were an employment at the relevant time. These matters can lead to disputes arising as to whether the invention was created during the course of employment or not, or whether the employee invented outside of their normal or specifically assigned employment duties, and devised aspects of the invention outside of the employment under which the employer claims the right to the patent. In this book it will shall seek to explain how to understand the consequences of these issues, by explaining how inventorship works and who is entitled to seek a patent for an invention.

1.2. The law of patents provides for the protection of inventions, and in the UK this is governed by the Patents Act 1977.

Though it is worth noting that as the UK is part of the European Patent Convention (EPC), it is possible to obtain a patent covering the UK via an application to the European Patent Office. The EPC being a unitary system of applying for patents in one place which results in an ability to obtain a number of patents, one for each jurisdiction participating in the convention. There is no such thing as a European Patent *per se*, it is shorthand to refer to a simplified system of obtaining nationally granted patents in each jurisdiction that are signatories to the EPC.

1.3. Any person, either alone or jointly with another, may make an application for a patent—whether for a national patent under the Patents Act 1977 Act, or a European patent application in accordance with the EPC. An international application, similar in some ways to the EPC system, in accordance with the Patent Co-operation Treaty is also possible, and may be made by a resident or national of a contracting state, and the UK is a contracting state. Via these systems an invention may be protected across the globe provided it meets the requirements for granting a patent in each jurisdiction.

1.4. The first part of the UK law to understand when considering employee inventions is s.39 of the Patents Act. It provides that an invention made by an employee belongs to the employer if made 'in the course of the normal duties of the employee or in the course of duties falling outside his normal duties, but specifically assigned to him, and the circumstances in either case were such that an invention might reasonably be expected to result from the carrying out of his duties.' The law also considers where you work as s.81 states that s.39 only applies if the employee was mainly employed in the UK, or if the employer had a place of business in the UK to which the employee was attached and the employee was not mainly employed in another country – s.43(2).

1.5. The purpose of this chapter is to highlight certain issues of importance, that it may help to consider if you are determining whether an invention is an employee invention or not. When determining if an invention belongs to an employer, there are three questions to ask: (1) What were the normal duties of the employee, (2) what, if any, specific duties were assigned and (3) might an invention have resulted and if so then might it be expected? The answers to those questions if showing that the invention was devised from the employee's duties and an invention might be expected to confirm that the invention belongs to the employer.

1.6. There can be circumstances however, where the employee has carried out work with others (whether fellow employees, external contractors, or others they know who are not connected to the employer). For example, if a business relies on employees working alongside independent contractors to conduct research and to invent new products, is the correct contractual structure in place so as to be clear as to the ownership of any resultant invention? If the independent contractor is, for example, the inventor, the ownership may not be solely that of the commissioning business, unless the engagement contract makes this clear. Answering these questions assists in understanding who is entitled to apply for a patent.

1.7. The employee invention, whilst starting with a natural assumption that their invention will be owned by their employer, is only a starting place. Whether an invention is one created by an employee, and the nature of the relationship between the person believed to be an employee and their employer, turns on facts. Only when you are sure of the facts and relationship can you determine who owns an invention.

CHAPTER TWO
GENERAL SUMMARY

2.1. It is probably a matter of common sense to most people, that if one person employs another to create, then the employer should, without too much formality, get the fruits of that employee's efforts. In much the same way that a company responsible for building a bridge owes nothing to its actual builders except remuneration for work – in one sense the bridge was built by the company, in another by its workers. The rationale for this vertical transfer of ownership, arises because unless businesses are able to obtain the benefit of creations then valuable investment will not be made. Therefore the argument goes that an employee gains benefits by way of pay (in various guises), job security, health insurance, worker cooperation and so on in return.

2.2. Under the Wilson and then the Callaghan Governments, towards the end of the 1970s when the Patents Bill was being debated in Parliament and, allegedly, during the beer and sandwiches discussions at Downing Street, representations were said to be made by worker's representatives that, whilst the employer expropriation model of creations was correct, the inventive employee, employed to invent (or not being employed to invent but does so none-the-less and assigns rights to the employer), should is some cases, where exceptional benefits accrued, gain a slice of the cake and should not be content with their pay packet. This led to the enactment of sections 40 and 41, designed to compensate employee inventors in certain circumstances.

2.3. Towards the end of the 1990s, it was becoming clear that the courts, applying normal rules of statutory construction, were not being as generous towards those employees as was originally envisaged. This led to amendment of sections 40 and 41. The original scenario was that where an employee created an invention, for which a patent has been granted, and where that patent was of outstanding benefit to the employer (having regard to the size of the employer and the nature of its business) then specific compensation rules applied. This was changed at the beginning of 2005 so that where an employee created an invention, for which a patent has been granted, and where that patent or the corresponding invention was of outstanding benefit to the employer (having regard to the size of the employer and the nature of its business) then specific compensation rules applied. Although it appeared to be a subtle change, in practice it was believed by the Government of the day that the result would be that more employee compensation would be allowed. The general consensus is that the amendments to s.40 of the Patents Act has made it easier to make a claim for compensation. However many also believe that is only applicable to patents granted after 2005, and as the true value of a patent tends to be realised toward the end of its 20 year monopoly, there have yet to be enough cases to know if this is correct. Therefore, in summary it is still too early to tell whether this is the case.

2.4. It was also envisaged that in certain cases the criteria for employee rewards, and whether they were available, could be codified by agreement between unions and employers (referred to as a 'relevant collective agreement'). As a result, if a relevant collective agreement was in place then it replaced the entitlement rules in s.40. This was sensible. Specific industries work in specific ways, which may require specialist negotiation, which anything but lengthy and probably wordy legislation would otherwise not be able to deal with.

2.5. If the compensation rules applied then the court awarding compensation had to have regard to certain principles in s.41, though principles being dictated by the notion of fairness (as in a 'fair' share of the benefit accruing to the employer). The 'share' in question is a share of the benefit accruing and the benefit that may be reasonably expected to accrue from either direct exploitation of or from assignment away on a closed company basis. In other words, employers could not avoid the obligation to pay compensation by mere dint of assigning the patent to a subsidiary. The employer also needs to fairly reflect the benefit accrued in the compensation to the employee. The level of compensation was then calculated by having regard to the employee's duties, the effort and skills exercised and other relevant inputs, as discussed further in this text.

CHAPTER THREE
THE RELATIONSHIP BETWEEN EMPLOYER AND EMPLOYEE, THE NOTION OF A WORKER AND THE INVENTIVE CONTRIBUTION

3.1. Whether a person is an employer is usually not a matter of much dispute. An employer is any person who engages another to perform work of any description. An employee is harder to define. The notion of employment is not anywhere perfectly defined but it is best stated as; employment is working for another in return for remuneration, where the employer directs their activity until the relationship comes to an end by some means. Even then problems arise where, especially in today's gig economy, a person has a number of jobs, though just because a person does have a number of jobs does not deny them of the right to call themselves or be called an employee.

Does Employment Law need to be understood?

3.2. Employment law has had to grapple with evolving terminology such as the notion of a worker being distinct to that of an employee, but patent law has not. It therefore remains to be seen if the growing distinction of working relationships that are not 'employee' relationships could be used a way to question whether under the patent act an invention created by a 'worker' who is not an employee' interferes with the operation of the transfer form employee to employer of ownership.

3.3. Employment law explains an employee in the Employment Rights Act 1996 – section 230, as:

> (1) An employee means an individual who has entered into or works under (or, where the employment has ceased, worked under) a contract of employment.

> (2) A contract of employment means a contract of service or apprenticeship, whether express or implied, and (if it is express) whether oral or in writing.

3.4. For patent purposes an employee is defined in s.130(1) Patents Act 1977 by reference to a 'contract of employment,' and so it is similar to the employee definition in s.230(1) Employment Rights Act 1996.

3.5. Section 130 in the relevant part says –

> [An] 'employee' means a person who works or (where the employment has ceased) worked under a contract of employment or in employment under or for the purposes of a government department [or a person who serves (or served) in the naval, military or air forces of the Crown];

> [An] 'employer,' in relation to an employee, means the person by whom the employee is or was employed.

3.6. It may seem an easy question to answer as to whether someone is an employee. Most commonly, it is a person whose work is under a contract for a known employer. However, there are scenarios where an employee may have more than one job and in those circumstances if the jobs for different employers are similar, then it is sensible to be alive to what the employee is learning in each job and not to assume that their invention derived solely from working for your business. People who are part of your work force may operate as a consultant often expressed in terms of how they receive their remuneration, but depending on what their service contract agreement says, and the facts, they may or may not be capable of being an employee.

3.7. Similarly, a temporary 'worker' if they are for example a volunteer may not be an employee, depending on the circumstances. Therefore, workers and employees may not be the same. The definition of 'worker' in s.230(3) Employment Rights Act 1996, tells us that employees are a sub-group of 'workers' and so not all workers are employees. Section 230 of the Employment Rights Act 1996 states that:

(1) In this Act 'employee' means an individual who has entered into or works under (or, where the employment has ceased, worked under) a contract of employment.

(2) In this Act 'contract of employment' means a contract of service or apprenticeship, whether express or implied, and (if it is express) whether oral or in writing.

3.8. The term 'worker' is defined by section 230(3) of the 1996 Act, which states:

(3) In this Act 'worker' (except in the phrases 'shop worker' and 'betting worker') means an individual who has entered into or works under (or, where the employment has ceased, worked under) –

(a) A contract of employment, or

(b) Any other contract, whether express or implied and (if it is express) whether oral or in writing, whereby the individual undertakes to do or perform personally any work or services for another party to the contract whose status is not by virtue of the contract that of a client or customer of any profession or business undertaking carried on by the individual;

and any reference to a worker's contract shall be construed accordingly.

3.9. The same definition of a worker appears in Regulation 2(1) of the Working Time Regulations 1998. It is this concept of 'worker' from European Union law that has led the UK courts and tribunals to have to consider if an employee and worker are distinct. It is currently unclear how much may be derived from viewing the distinction between worker and employee and in the commentary which follows the distinction may not matter. However, it is also the case that the position of a worker has not been the subject of consideration in a patent entitlement context.

3.10. How to determine who is employed was considered in Ready Mixed Concrete (South East) Ltd v Ministry of Pensions and National Insurance [1968] 2 QB 497; it established that you can be under a contract to provide a service and not be an employee, even though much of the manner in which you provide those services makes you appear as an employee, in that scenario you are a worker because you are not under an employment contract. Accordingly, workers are those working for an entity but not under a contract of employment where their services are governed by other arrangements or terms and this can preclude employment rights. The distinction was considered by the Court of Appeal and the Supreme Court, in Autoclenz Ltd v Belcher [2009] EWCA Civ 1046 and [2011] UKSC 41. The case confirmed that the true relationship will be considered to determine if a person is an employee and you cannot simply say a person is not an employee in a contract and avoid employment rights, the true situation entitles the court to conclude a person was an employee. The point to note is that if the inventor is not an employee, then the provision in section 39 of the Patent Act 1977 that states a patent belongs to the employer will not guarantee ownership.

3.11. The relationship of the inventor to the business is therefore important, and others who are important contributors to the business but not employees need consideration, for example directors of a company. Directors are not necessarily employees, as Halsbury's Laws of England, explains:

> "A company director is an office-holder who is not, without more, an employee of the company. A director who actually works for the company, especially under a service agreement, may, however, also be an employee of the company..." (Parsons v Parsons [1979] F.S.R.254).

3.12. In those cases one must first determine if there is a contract at all, and then, if so, whether the contract is one 'of service' (i.e. employment) or 'for services' (i.e. provided on a self-employed basis). The question is one of law, and also the facts of the case in question (Davies v Presbyterian Church of Wales [1986] 1 W.L.R. 323; [1986] I.R.L.R. 194 HL).

3.13. Partners are another kind of person that are not automatically treated in the same way as employees. An equity-holding partner in a firm is an employer of the firm's staff and unless the partnership agreement says otherwise, they cannot be treated in the same manner as an employee when considering entitlement to inventions. The mere ownership of shares in a company, even by a majority shareholder, is also not relevant as the company is an entity quite separate from its members (Salomon v Salomon & Co Ltd [1897] A.C. 22 HL). The courts may be willing to look beyond the wording of any contracts to determine whether a person is self-employed or an employee, and will look at the actual relationship—see Autoclenz (above) and subsequent cases such as Pimlico Plumbers Ltd v Smith[2017] EWCA Civ 51; and Uber v Aslam [2018] EWCA Civ2748, but the outcomes will be and often tend to be fact specific. It is therefore sensible to consider what the intended arrangements should be for directors or partners and seek to put the question beyond doubt in written agreements with the business.

How does patent law define employees?

3.14. Whilst employment law shows it has grappled with issues of definition and relationships that fall outside a clear example of the employee and employer, the common law relied on in patent matters has a simple and elegant solution: In any specific employment context, as stated by Bristow J. in *Withers* v. *Flackwell Heath Football Supporters' Club* [1981] 1 I.R.L.R. 307, EAT, it depends upon the proper answer to the question "are you your own boss?" If the question is answered in the affirmative then the person is not an employee, otherwise an employment relationship exists. In some cases there will be evidence which is consistent with employment, such as contracts, PAYE slips and so on, but these could be conveniences, and are never conclusive in favour of a relationship of employment. The essence is one of control. However each case has its own facts, as was said by the then Lord Justice Denning in *Stevenson Jordan & Harrison Ltd* v. *Macdonald & Evans* [1952] 1 T.L.R. 101 at 111 said, distinguishing between a contract of service (*i.e.* employment) and a contract for service (*i.e.* not):-

> "It is almost impossible to give a precise definition of the distinction. It is often easy to recognise the contract of service when you see it but difficult to say where in the difference lies. A ship's master, a chauffeur, and a reporter on the staff of a newspaper are all employed under a contract of service; but a ships pilot, a taxi man, and a newspaper contributor are employed under contract for service."

3.15. In *Hall (Inspector of Taxes)* v. *Lorimer* [1992] 1 W.L.R. 939, [1992] S.T.C. 599, [1992] I.C.R. 739, (1992) 136 S.J.L.B. 175, *The Times*, June 4, 1992, Mummery J, stated ([1992] 1 W.L.R. 944) that the test was a matter of impression and could not be the subject of checklists:-

> "In order to decide whether a person carries on business on his own account it is necessary to consider many different aspects of that person's work activity. This is not a mechanical exercise of running through items on a check list to see whether they are present in, or absent from, a given situation. The object of the exercise is to paint a picture from the accumulation of detail. The overall effect can only be appreciated by standing back from the detailed picture which has been painted, by viewing it from a distance and by making an informed, considered, qualitative appreciation of the whole. It is a matter of eval-

uation of the overall effect of the detail, which is not necessarily the same as the sum total of the individual details. Not all details are of equal weight or importance in any given situation. The details may also vary in importance from one situation to another."

3.16. It can be seen from *Hall* v. *Lorimer*, that what the court was concerned with was; whether a person was self-employed (in which case one tax treatment applied), or to use the language of Mummery J., that person was "[A] person [who] carried on business on his own account" or whether a person was an employee (in which case a different tax treatment applied). It appears that being one rules out the other, but that Mummery J. suggests that each case is very much dependent upon its own facts. This is unsurprising if a little difficult to deal with in marginal cases.

3.17. In contradistinction is the notion of a worker, which is inherited or transposed as a notion of EU law into our domestic law. Recent cases involving the gig economy have explored this question, as to whether, if a person is a worker then rights set out in the Employment Rights Act 1996, the Working Time Regulations 1998 and the National Minimum Wage Act 1998 apply. However a 'worker' for those purposes is possibly (but not, sadly, conclusively) a sub-species of employee who has a contract for or of services and the recent cases on the gig economy are nothing to the points made above (see (1) *Uber B.V.*, (2) *Uber London Limited*, (3) *Uber Britannia Limited* v. (1) *Yaseen Aslam*, (2) *James Farrar*, (3) *Robert Dawson and Others* [2018] EWCA Civ 2748; [2019] 3 All E.R. 489; [2019] R.T.R. 25;, [2019] I.C.R. 845; [2019] I.R.L.R. 257; *The Times*, January 28, 2019, C.A.). It does remain to be established as to whether a person is can be defined as a worker but not be an employee. However, given Mummery J.'s test – so far as it is a test (perhaps approach might be a better word) – this must necessarily be an open question.

3.18. So much for the big test. One might ask what have the courts, faced with the problem, actually found? Unfortunately it is difficult to answer this question in a comprehensive way since the Mummery approach is intentionally broad brush and, although affirmed by the Court of Appeal ([1994] 1 W.L.R. 209;L [1994] 1 All E.R. 250; [1994] S.T.C. 23; [1994] I.C.R. 218; [1994] I.R.L.R. 171; 66 T.C. 349; [1993] S.T.I. 1382; (1993) 90(45) L.S.G. 45; (1993) 137 S.J.L.B. 256; *The Times*, November 18, 1993, *The Independent*, November 15, 1993), the approach is easy to state but necessarily gives no clues in its application. Indeed the Court of Appeal in *Hall* v. *Lorimer* itself was unable to resist giving a little guidance by stating that; whilst each case did depend upon its own facts what might be of significance was the degree of dependence of the employee on a particular paymaster, though even that might be too much. An independent contractor, such as a business rescue specialist, may move from job to job but only have one job at any one time. This was derived from the case of *Market Investigations Ltd* v. *Minister of Social Security* [1969] 2 Q.B. 173; [1969] 2 W.L.R. 1; [1968] 3 All E.R. 732; [2010] B.T.C. 103; (1968) 112 S.J. 905, C.A., where a person was periodically engaged. On each occasion of work fixed remuneration was agreed. The job required to be done was accompanied by detailed instructions and a certain number of days' work within a given time was required, though there was no provision for sick pay or for holidays. Further, the notional employer was of the view that it could not dismiss the notional employee. On the question of whether the notional employer had to make national insurance (NI) contributions (which would be the case if there was an employment relationship) or whether it was down to the notional employee alone, the Court of Appeal stated that the crucial facts to be considered were the extent and degree of control exercised by the notional employer over the notional employee when viewed at in the context of the engagement, and now employment, contract in the whole.

3.19. It goes without saying that the existence of a contract, the right to give specific directions, the exclusive nature of the relationship and even the attitude of the notional employee may all be relevant considerations. However, it is not something which the relevant parties can simply choose for themselves, simply by creating a context or a contractual situation, whether genuine or contrived – reality matters.

3.20. What is the test for employer expropriation? *i.e.* In what circumstances does an employment relationship, once established, give rise to a right on the part of an employer to expropriate the fruits of the inventive labours of the employee? The question is stated in s39, which repays quoting in full:-

Right to employees' inventions.

39. (1) Notwithstanding anything in any rule of law, an invention made by an employee shall, as between him and his employer, be taken to belong to his employer for the purposes of this Act and all other purposes if—

(*a*) it was made in the course of the normal duties of the employee or in the course of duties falling outside his normal duties, but specifically assigned to him, and the circumstances in either case were such that an invention might reasonably be expected to result from the carrying out of his duties; or

(*b*) the invention was made in the course of the duties of the employee and, at the time of making the invention, because of the nature of his duties and the particular responsibilities arising from the nature of his duties he had a special obligation to further the interests of the employer's undertaking.

(2) Any other invention made by an employee shall, as between him and his employer, be taken for those purposes to belong to the employee.

(3) Where by virtue of this section an invention belongs, as between him and his employer, to an employee, nothing done—

(*a*) by or on behalf of the employee or any person claiming under him for the purposes of pursuing an application for a patent, or

(*b*) by any person for the purpose of performing or working the invention,

shall be taken to infringe any copyright or design right to which, as between him and his employer, his employer is entitled in any model or document relating to the invention."

3.21. The words in the introductory part of sub-section (1) are significant, and require a little explanation. The words

"Notwithstanding anything in any rule of law" for instance mean that s.36(1) overrides anything which may be described as a rule of law, such as a statutory provision or a judicial declaration as to law, though it was unclear whether a rule of law includes a rule of equity, though following *Xtralite (Rooflights) Ltd* v. *Hartington Conway Ltd* [2003] E.W.H.C. 1872; [2004] R.P.C. 161; (2003) 100(37) L.S.G. 33; *The Times*, October 1, 2003, Pumfrey J. a rule of law does include a rule of equity. The declaratory part of the subsection then states that an "invention made by an employee shall ... be taken to belong to [the] ... employer for the purposes of this Act and all other purposes;" this part is relatively straightforward but the words qualifying the declaration by stating that it applies only in situations arising as 'between' employer and employee are a little opaque. What they mean is that if any point on the relationship is to be taken, then the only people who are bound by sub-section (1) are the notional employer and the notional employee, it being open to any other in appropriate circumstances to take the or any wider point should it arise. It may arise in situations where the employee has expropriated relevant information so as to enable the invention to be made or there is some other legal means of interfering with title to the invention. What this means is cryptic until one has regard to the inventorship principle which is; that an inventor always has the first right – though that right might be displaced in certain circumstances, which are discussed later – to apply for a patent. Therefore where an employee being an inventor, derives the first right to apply, that right is displaced as between the employee and employer in favour of the employment rule. However, that set of rules does not displace some outsider third party from claiming that they are the real inventor or are somehow otherwise entitled. Neither does it disentitle an outsider from claiming that the rela-

tionship in question is not an employer-employee relationship but only if that outsider has a claim to be entitled in
some way. Where this employer-employee relationship does
not exist then the employee is entitled. However, there is a
little more to sub-section (1) than this, as will be dealt with
below.

3.22. As an example: Mr. Worker is employed by Mr. Boss or; Mr.
Worker works with Mr. Other, who is not a relevant
employee, and they jointly come up with an invention. Thus
Mr. Worker and Mr. Other are joint inventors and they are
entitled, jointly, to apply for a patent. However, as between
Mr. Worker and Mr. Boss, Mr. Boss is entitled, hence whilst
Mr. Worker and Mr. Other are joint inventors, Mr. Boss and
Mr. Other are the joint applicants for any patent of the
invention. Mr. Other then contends that for some reason,
Mr. Worker and Mr. Boss are not in a relevant employment
relationship. However, Mr. Other's position as applicant is
unaltered, no matter whether Mr. Worker or Mr. Boss are
also joint applicants. Mr. Other can do nothing.

3.23. Not all employment counts: The invention must be the
product of the employee acting in the course of his normal or
specifically assigned duties, and where inventions might reasonably be expected to result from the carrying out of those
duties. Thus mere employment without more will not do. It
needs to be proven that the employee was working within
some sphere (either as part of normal duties of specifically
instructed) where inventions might reasonably be expected to
result. It is irrelevant that the employee came up with the
invention in company time or used company facilities to
come up with the invention in question. It is likewise irrelevant that the employee committed legal wrongs in doing
those things. A researcher working in a research department,

would clearly fit the bill in relation to every product of the work carried out by that researcher since research often leads to new things, though even then only of inventions are reasonably expected to result. If inventions are not expected to result, but nevertheless do, then the right to expropriate is lost unless some other means of expropriation can be found. Therefore, the burden on the employer seeking to expropriate the invention of an office cleaner who invents is very heavy indeed.

3.24. In some cases, circumstances arise where an employee has an obligation to further the interests of his employer, even though there was no obligation to invent or expectation that inventions might result. This kind of situation usually arises in the higher echelons of management. A head of a research department, for instance may have the responsibility of determining the direction of research so as to maximise profits and profitability, this could con note with an obligation to further the employer's interests, a situation arising under s.39(1)(b).

3.25. The situation arising under s.39(1)(b) is not to be confused with the obligations on those at the highest echelons of management – members of the board or (possibly) large shareholders – especially those the subject of a shareholders agreement, who can have duties of care to the corporate entity. Directors and shareholders are often not employees of their organisation but do have duties not to allow conflicts to arise. In those circumstances the director may be under an obligation to account for their inventions to their company irrespective of s39 (see, for instance *Ultraframe (UK) Ltd* v. *Clayton* (m 2) and *Ultraframe UK Ltd* v. *Fielding* (m 2) [2003] E.W.C.A. Civ 1805; [2004] E.C.D.R. 34; [2004]

R.P.C. 24; (2004) 101(5) L.S.G. 29; *The Times*, January 12, 2004, C.A.).

3.26. In some cases, the question arises as to whether the contribution is joint. In this regard the speech of Lord Hoffmann in *Yeda Research and Development Co Ltd v. Rhône-Poulenc Rorer International Holdings Inc* [2007] UKHL 43 (HL); [2008] R.P.C. 1, H.L. repays setting out:-

> "20. The inventor is defined in ... [the Patents Act 1977] as "the actual deviser of the invention". The word "actual" denotes a contrast with a deemed or pretended deviser of the invention; it means, as Laddie J. said in *University of Southampton's Applications* [2005] R.P.C. 11, [39], the natural person who "came up with the inventive concept." It is not enough that someone contributed to the claims, because they may include non-patentable integers derived from prior art: see *Henry Brothers (Magherafelt) Ltd v. Ministry of Defence* [1997] R.P.C. 693, 706; [1999] R.P.C. 442, Jacob J. As Laddie J. said in the *University of Southampton* case, the "contribution must be to the formulation of the inventive concept". Deciding upon inventorship will therefore involve assessing the evidence adduced by the parties as to the nature of the inventive concept and who contributed to it. In some cases this may be quite complex because the inventive concept is a relationship of discontinuity between the claimed invention and the prior art. Inventors themselves will often not know exactly where it lies.
>
> 21. ... [A] person who seeks to be added as a joint inventor bears the burden of proving that he contributed to the inventive concept underlying the claimed invention and a person who seeks to be substituted as sole inventor

bears the additional burden of proving that the inventor named in the patent did not contribute to the inventive concept. But that, in my opinion, is all. The ... [Patents Act 1977] is the code for determining entitlement and there is nothing in the ... [Patents Act 1977] which says that entitlement depends upon anything other than being the inventor. There is no justification, in a dispute over who was the inventor, to import questions of whether one claimant has some personal cause of action against the other."

3.27. As Lord Hoffmann points out, this can be a potentially difficult exercise; to answer an easy question – who came up with the inventive concept (or *et derived inventivum conceptu*)? A loyal, able and dutiful technician, who worked hard to enable the invention of his master and without whom the inventor would not have been able to progress his ideas, yet is not entitled, valuable though the contribution may be. If that technician makes suggestions, then even that will not be enough to be a devisor and therefore inventor, without more. If, however the suggestions, which appear as part of the final invention are inventive then the technician, at long last, gets a look in, <u>but only if that technician contributes to the inventive concept</u>. So if the technician provides something inventive to a claim, but not to the inventive concept, then the technician has not done enough to be an inventor. To emphasise: It is important to look at the overall inventive concept in question when examining this question. Say that our inventor, as a result of inventive thought, comes up with a new non-steroidal anti-inflammatory drug, then the invention whose inventive concept is centred around the molecule (essentially a structure) is that of the solo inventor. If the technician however comes up with a novel and inventive way of *making* the compound, then that is a different invention and not part of the original inventive concept. Each gets their own invention and their own right to apply for a patent (a product patent in the first case and a process one in the second).

3.28. In many cases the contributions are indistinguishable and the court will not examine these questions too carefully. What happens though if a specific contribution is made in relation to a specific aspect of the invention, but which adds noting to the inventive concept? In that case, the specific contribution is helpful but irrelevant. As Lord Hoffmann said "[I]t is not enough that someone contributed to the claims, because they may include non-patentable integers derived from prior art." If, however, it appears that there are two inventive concepts appearing in one application then it is open for one of the joint inventors to apply to the patent granting authority (the UK Intellectual Property Office) have two patent applications proceed separately.

CHAPTER FOUR
EMPLOYEE INVENTIONS ARISING UNDER THE PATENTS ACT 1977 AND THE EUROPEAN PATENTS CONVENTION

4.1. The primary starting point is s.7, which states:-

Right to apply for and obtain a patent.

7. (1) Any person may make an application for a patent either alone or jointly with another.

(2) A patent for an invention may be granted—

(*a*) primarily to the inventor or joint inventors;

(*b*) in preference to the foregoing, to any person or persons who, by virtue of any enactment or rule of law, or any foreign law or treaty or international convention, or by virtue of an enforceable term of any agreement entered into with the inventor before the making of the invention, was or were at the time of the making of the invention entitled to the whole of the property in it (other than equitable interests) in the United Kingdom;

(*c*) in any event, to the successor or successors in title of any person or persons mentioned in paragraph (*a*) or (*b*) above or any person so mentioned and the successor or successors in title of another person so mentioned; and to no other person.

(3) In this Act "inventor" in relation to an invention means the actual deviser of the invention and "joint inventor" shall be construed accordingly.

(4) Except so far as the contrary is established, a person who makes an application for a patent shall be taken to be the person who is entitled under subs(2) above to be granted a patent and two or more persons who make such an application jointly shall be taken to be the persons so entitled."

4.2. There is a requirement in certain cases for the court, when construing parts of the Patents Act 1977, to have regard to certain treaties and international conventions. This is set out in s.130(7), so that, for instance, when considering parts of s.1 concerning validity, the court must ensure conformity with the European Patent Convention (EPC), the Community Patent Convention (CPC) and the Patent Co-operation Treaty. It is not required under s.130(7), however, for s.7 to be construed in this way, in other words, s.7 is free standing and is to be construed in accordance with standard rules on statutory construction.

4.3. A number of observations may be made about s.7, the first and foremost being that a sole inventor and a joint inventor are concepts which the law of patents recognises. This means that the inventor or joint inventors are the individuals entitled to apply as applicants or joint applicants. The first rule may be displaced by a second rule in preference to the first rule, that a person (or persons, as the case may be) is deemed to be entitled because:

4.3.1. A law or treaty says so; that 'law' includes any foreign law, rule of law (including any rule contained in the

Patents Act 1977 itself) or treaty or international convention BUT ONLY IF that law cedes entitlement to "the whole of the property in [that invention]" to another or

4.3.2. The inventor entered into an appropriate and enforceable contract before the making of the invention, to yield to another, at the time of the making of the invention entitled to "the whole of the property in [that invention]." The contract rule does not apply to equitable interests arising as a result of that contract. In the converse though equitable interests apart from those arising as a result of a contract might enable a person in the position of a beneficiary to claim the right to apply for the patent if that claim in equity could be equated with a rule of law.

4.4. **Illustration:** Consider a person who invents a new and inventive way of monitoring heartbeats. The monitoring device they devise may be worn as part of a watch and they are entitled to apply for a GB patent under the first rule. However, the inventor comes from Ruritania and the 'Ruritanian Patents Act 1977' states that any spouse is entitled to apply for a patent if at the time of making the invention they are married to any Ruritanian who is entitled to apply for a patent anywhere in the world. Under Ruritanian law the husband and wife are entitled to apply jointly for a GB patent since a foreign law says so, even though under UK patent law they are not because the other person has to be entitled to the whole of the property in the invention and not the right to apply for a patent with their spouse. So as the Ruritanian law states that both the husband and wife are jointly entitled to the whole of the property in the invention then they may both apply for a GB patent.

4.5. The EPC apart it is not believed that there are any foreign laws, rules of law (the rules of equity apart, which are dealt with below) which impact on this question. The EPC (at article 60) is not entirely congruent with s.7. Article 60 EPC states:-

> "60. (1) The right to a ... [patent granted in accordance with the EPC and designated a member state designation – a European Patent -] shall belong to the inventor or his successor in title. If the inventor is an employee, the right to a European patent shall be determined in accordance with the law of the State in which the employee is mainly employed; if the State in which the employee is mainly employed cannot be determined, the law to be applied shall be that of the State in which the employer has the place of business to which the employee is attached.

> (2) If two or more persons have made an invention independently of each other, the right to a European patent therefor shall belong to the person whose European patent application has the earliest date of filing, provided that this first application has been published.

> (3) In proceedings before the European Patent Office, the applicant shall be deemed to be entitled to exercise the right to a European patent."

4.6. Article 60 EPC is no more than a broad statement of how the EPO understands the law relating to inventors and their employers (though the matter is not one for the EPO). Section 7 on the other hand requires the external provision in question to operate in some positive way so as to make another person entitled to the "the whole of the property in [that invention]." Looked at this way, art. 60 EPC does not have this effect and so is not relevant. The conclusion therefore is that s.7(2)(b) is unlikely ever to be a problem so far as international treaties are concerned.

4.7. Section 7(2)(c) is more straightforward. If a person, such as a contract research organisation (often known as an CRO) is contracted to invent, before the invention is devised and does invent, then provided that the contract makes provision for the property in the invention to become that of the commissioning party, the right to apply for a patent in relation to that invention resides with the commissioning party.

4.8. **Illustration:** Consider where A and B enter into an enforceable heads of agreement whereby B is to carry out certain technical research for A and which states 'inventions by B in the technical area shall be the property of A.' In consequence B is greeting to transfer the whole of the property in the invention to A and thus A can apply for a patent in the UK.

4.9. The foregoing applies to patents applied for in the UK, at the UK IPO. However, the position relating to applicants for patents in the EPO is more complicated. Matters of title (including matters of entitlement to apply for a patent) are a matter for each national patent granting authority to determine. The EPO will not get involved in those questions. Further, where an issue of entitlement arises in relation to an EPO granted patent which has led to a national patent then there is provision for making an application to the UKIPO to correct the position but only so far as concerns the GB patent. That much is straightforward. The issue is more complicated where the wrong applicant has applied; where, for instance, the CRO in the illustration given above has made an application for a patent in the EPO and the EPO patent is pending but not granted. The EPO will not entertain representations and, further, there may be a whole set of national rules as to who is entitled once the EPC patent becomes a national patent. The rules in this respect are not harmonised and the true applicant may have to wait in the side lines until grant (and suffer any prosecution strategies which the applicant may choose to render) and then make a number of national applications in each of the states in which the EPO patent became a national one.

4.10. In the UK, concerning patents emanating from the EPO (though not yet granted), there is some respite from this complicated situation; it works to divide the situation into two (though only for the purposes of deciding jurisdiction), being those instances where the argument is about employment (often known as an employer-employee question) and other cases. Further, the UK system for not only EPO cases, but in all respects will only intervene (though if it does then the right to do so is exclusive of other authorities – *Innovia Films Limited* v. *Frito-Lay North America Inc.* [2012] E.W.H.C. 790; [2012] R.P.C. 557, Arnold J.) if the would-be applicant is resident or has their principal place of business in the United Kingdom, or the actual applicant is in the same situation – it is not an open shop. The jurisdiction of the UKIPO is set out in s12 (the comptroller being the person who has authority to decide these matters):-

12. (1) At any time before a patent is granted for an invention in pursuance of an application made under the

law of any country other than the United Kingdom or under any treaty or international convention (whether or not that application has been made)—

(a) any person may refer to the comptroller the question whether he is entitled to be granted (alone or with any other persons) any such patent for that invention or has or would have any right in or under any such patent or an application for such a patent; or

(b) any of two or more co-proprietors of an application for such a patent for that invention may so refer the question whether any right in or under the application should be transferred or granted to any other person;

and the comptroller shall determine the question so far as he is able to and may make such order as he thinks fit to give effect to the determination."

4.11. Importantly the application must be made before the patent is granted. Equally importantly the statutory jurisdiction rules work only in relation to EPO patent applications (though strictly that may be regarded as a basket of national applications – the position remains untested); the position regarding other foreign patents is subject to the more general rules on jurisdiction. If the patent is granted then the right to apply to correct the position is more limited and the right in relation to foreign patents as opposed to foreign applications is lost. S.12 is superficially useful but is often costly to engage. The Comptroller of Patents, Designs and Trade Marks will want to be given evidence of the patent laws of other countries involved, which can be expensive. If the Comptroller of Patents, Designs and Trade Marks deems that the application would be better dealt with in court then the

Comptroller of Patents, Designs and Trade Marks can refer the matter to the court. Further, under s.82 the matter under s.12 will only be entertained of the applicant has a residence or principal place of business in the UK or, if not so (and in addition where the applicant has no place of business or residence in any of the other EPC contracting states), where the opposing party has a principal place of business or residence in the UK <u>and</u> that opposing party claims to be entitled.

4.12. In relation to employer-employee questions the rules are the same. In either the employer-employee case or in other cases the Comptroller of Patents, Designs and Trade Marks will cede jurisdiction to other patent offices if there is a written agreement agreeing to submit to that other jurisdiction.

4.13. The foregoing applies to situations, which arise before the relevant patent application has made it to grant. Afterwards though and whilst the entitlement proceedings are on foot the person claiming entitlement has to take the matter up with each national patent office. The position concerning patent applications, which were granted during the process, appears to be that any proceedings under s.12 are halted midway, though there is no judicial decision which examines this question.

4.14. In cases of a purely domestic nature, the position is also governed by the Patents Act 1977, but this time s8 and applies only to UK applications. In this case, the jurisdiction is not limited to place of business or employment issues. Further, if the application proceeds to grant whilst the s8 process is underway then the application is converted to a s.37 application.

4.15. Under s37 the procedure enables a person claiming to be properly entitled to apply for a declaration that this is so. There is a large amount of corrective machinery in sections 8, 12 and 37 to enable the true applicant to get rights without being prejudiced by priority issues. Further, in some cases the application may be divided into two (because there are in fact two inventive concepts). Again, corrective machinery exists to preserve priority rights. Importantly, if s.37 is invoked then the Comptroller of Patents, Designs and Trade Marks only has jurisdiction if the entitlement application is made within two years from the date of grant of the patent, unless it is shown that the patentee or subsequent assignee knew either (i) at the time of the grant or (ii) at the time of the transfer of the patent to the assignee that they were not entitled to the patent.

What is an employee?

4.16. The notion of an employee is not anywhere defined in statute law. This is deliberate since a multitude of circumstances can give rise to an employment relationship. What can be said is that an employee is a person who has an employment relationship with their employer.

4.17. The closet one gets in defining how an employment relationship exists for the purposes of patent law is in s.130(1), which speaks of a 'contract of employment.'

4.18. Section 130 in relevant part states –

> "[An] 'employee' means a person who works or (where the employment has ceased) worked under a contract of employment or in employment under or for the purposes

of a government department [or a person who serves (or served) in the naval, military or air forces of the Crown];

"[An] 'employer,' in relation to an employee, means the person by whom the employee is or was employed."

4.19. The Patents Act 1977 does not assist in knowing what constitutes a contract of employment. It is a fairly nebulous notion, though one which has been the subject of consideration by employment courts. It is, as lawyers would put it a common law idea to be decided by principles of circumstance and expedience

4.20. It may seem an easy question to answer as to whether someone is an employee of a particular employer. However, there are scenarios where the position is more complicated, as a matter of fact, where there are multiple employers, where job descriptions and duties overlap. In cases where a person is not acting as an employee then a contract will usually provide for any inventive bounty to be for the benefit of the person engaging the consultant; however it does not follow that in the absence of terms dealing with this that there is any rule which alienates the consultant from their invention. The stark reality is that unless a person is a relevant employee then anything they invent is in danger of remaining with that employee. This reality is tempered somewhat by the fact that in some circumstances where a contractor is engaged (but not on an employed basis) to invent then it might be implied into any contract of service that the benefit of any invention is to pass to the person engaging the contractor. However implying terms into contracts always carries risks. In *Bio Pure Technology* v. *Jarzon Plastics* BL/O/087/05, 31 March 2005 before the Comptroller of Patents, Designs and Trade Marks it was determined that on the facts of that case a term could be implied (in answering the rhetorical question, what else was he engaged to do, if not invent?) that the inventiveness of the consultant was something which was intended to benefit the person engaging him.

4.21. An employee might invent but the invention might not be within the duties assigned to them (either generally or specifically) or an invention might not be expected to result from the work of the employee. In those circumstances the employee retains the rights to any invention of theirs, even if carried out during employer time, using facilities provided by the employer.

4.22. Section 7(3) makes clear that an inventor or the joint inventors, in the case where there is more than one, in relation to an invention means the actual deviser or devisors (as the case may be) of the invention.

CHAPTER FIVE
EMPLOYEE INVENTIONS
ARISING IN EQUITY

5.1. The law of England and that of Wales is that strict statutory rights will not be required or insisted upon if it can be shown that reliance upon them would be unconscionable. However, since the law cannot re-write a statute or attenuate a common law rule it avoids the problem by creating legal rights and also beneficial or equitable rights and then creating rights and obligations between the two. Equitable rights can be as powerful as legal rights in some circumstances and can be nugatory in others. For instance, a land owner who gives land to another, receives money as the purchase price for that land, at market value, and behaves in all manners as if the land had been conveyed even though the necessary formalities had not been completed, will be bound in equity to observe what his conscience dictates and equity (or, more strictly, the rules of equity) will enable to court of equity to make orders to regularise the position, including corrective orders to ensure that the forgotten formalities are complied with. All equity asks in terms of its own formalities is that all concerned are properly before the court in some way, whether as claimant or defendant. In the land owner case the land owner remains the legal owner of the land and the land registry will record that, but the purchaser will become the beneficial owner and a relationship of trust will exist as between the land owner and the beneficiary (hence the expression 'trust'). The instances where a trust type relationship may exist are infinite and the cases are legion, often depending on the detail.

5.2. In relation to patents the rules of equity still operate and will or may become involved. However readers are warned; this might not be correct since the rules in s7(2) are fairly comprehensive and have been described by the House of Lords, no less, in *Yeda Research and Development Co Limited v. Rhone-Poulenc Rorer International Holdings Incorporated* [2008] R.P.C. 1, H.L. as, by Lord Hoffmann, an 'exhaustive code.' In addition s7(2) does appear to preclude equitable interests – a patent may be granted "to any person … who, by virtue of any … rule of law … was or were at the time of the making of the invention entitled to the whole of the property in … [the invention] (other than equitable interests) in the United Kingdom." However Lord Hoffmann left the door wide open by examining the case where one person invested in a particular technology but that somehow another who knew what was going by and stood by and who was technically entitled under s7(2). In that case, which gives rise to a legal construct known as proprietary estoppel – essentially equity intervening to stop this sort of unconscionable behaviour, Lord Hoffmann stated (at page 10) that "There is no reason why the equitable rules of proprietary estoppel should not apply to a patent in the same way as to any other property. The powers of the Comptroller of Patents, Designs and Trade Marks are expressed in terms wide enough to enable him to give effect to … [that] defence …"

5.3. To illustrate consider, a person, who is a director of a company, invents something, which would be of use to the company, though he is under no obligation to do so; in those circumstances the director owes a fiduciary duty to his company (the relationship being one of principal and agent) and the company is the beneficiary of those inventions, including having a right to call upon the director to vest title to it absolutely – *Ultraframe (UK) Limited v. Clayton (m 2) and Ultraframe UK Limited v. Fielding* (m 2) [2003] E.W.C.A. Civ 1805; [2004] E.C.D.R. 338; [2004] R.P.C. 479; (2004) 101(5) L.S.G. 29; The Times, January 12, 2004, C.A.

5.4. It is important to recognise though that a mere employee does not owe the same duties to his employer as a director does to his company (or other entity such as a partnership); the employment rules, though stricter, are more clearly defined. Conversely, a director whose acts are forgiven or ratified or otherwise approved of so that the company somehow relinquishes its claim to be the beneficial owner of the relevant rights walks away with the rights. What is important is that there has to be some positive process of lawful disengagement by the company. It should be recalled that mere dispositions of capital to directors for no consideration are usually unlawful unless sanctioned by the court.

Best Practice

5.5. Whilst equity may enable implied contracts and terms, it remains the better course to have the arrangements clearly documented to avoid disputes. Where working with a number of collaborators it is sensible to take legal advice on the best structures and contracts for the development of inventions.

CHAPTER SIX
EMPLOYEE INVENTIONS
AND ASSIGNMENTS

6.1. In some cases the employer and employee may negotiate an assignment of the patent or the rights in the invention from the employee to the employer. This is a request, often made in the context of international applications, as some patent prosecution offices prefer to see assignments, which simply repeat the true position between the employee and the employer. These assignments are sometimes termed; confirmatory assignments. However, this practice can raise issues. The issue most common is that the form of the 'confirmation' of assignment raises questions as to whether there was a valid assignment under the employment relationship without the further written assignment. Consequently, care is needed to ensure that in 'confirming' the position you do not question what went before.

6.2. Since the object of s.7 is to provide a compete code it seems that the assignment route is not one which s.7 envisages, but this would be wrong. If property is inalienable (*i.e.* cannot be assigned) then a law or rule must say so. The Patents Act 1977 is perfectly clear on the matter, that assignment of inventions, applications of patents and patents may be assigned at any stage. Section 30 is clear:-

Nature of, and transactions in, patents and applications for patents.

30. (1) Any patent or application for a patent is personal property (without being a thing in action), and any patent

or any such application and rights in or under it may be transferred, created or granted in accordance with subsections (2) to (7) below.

(2) Subject to s36(3) below [which deals with co-ownership and which requires all owners to act in the case of dispositions], any patent or any such application, or any right in it, may be assigned or mortgaged.

...

(6) Any of the following transactions, that is to say—

(*a*) any assignment or mortgage of a patent or any such application, or any right in a patent or any such application;

(*b*) any assent relating to any patent or any such application or right;

shall be void unless it is in writing and is signed [or sealed, as the case may be] by or on behalf of the assignor or mortgagor (or, in the case of an assent or other transaction by a personal representative, by or on behalf of the personal representative)."

6.3. Section 30(1) is of interest. As one can see a patent or an application for it is to be regarded as personal property without being a thing in action. What that means in English is that the rules concerning the formalities for assignments (that they have to be in writing and, in the case of a debt, that notice has to be provided to the debtor) are not applicable to patents or applications for patents. Instead, the rules in the Patents Act 1977 require that an assignment must be registered on the patents register and that constitutes the notice requirement. Failure to register an assignment in a timely fashion can lead to adverse costs consequence in legal proceedings. s68 sets out what those effects are:-

"Effect of non-registration on infringement proceedings.

68. Where by virtue of a transaction, instrument or event to which s33 above applies a person becomes the proprietor or one of the proprietors or an exclusive licensee of a patent and the patent is subsequently infringed before the transaction, instrument or event is registered, in [infringement] proceedings ..., the court or comptroller shall not award him costs ... unless—

(*a*) the transaction, instrument or event is registered within the period of six months beginning with its date; or

(*b*) the court or the comptroller is satisfied that it was not practicable to register the transaction, instrument or event before the end of that period and that it was registered as soon as practicable thereafter."

The 'instrument or event' referred to in s.68 (taken verbatim from s.33(6)) is

"(*a*) the assignment or assignation of a patent or application for a patent, or a right in it;

(*b*) the mortgage of a patent or application or the granting of security over it;

(*c*) the grant, assignment or assignation of a licence or sub-licence, or mortgage of a licence or sub-licence, under a patent or application;

(*d*) the death of the proprietor or one of the proprietors of any such patent or application or any person having a right in or under a patent or application and the vesting by an assent of personal representatives of a patent, application or any such right; and

(*e*) any order or directions of a court or other competent authority—

transferring a patent or application or any right in or under it to any person; or

that an application should proceed in the name of any person;

and in either case the event by virtue of which the court or authority had power to make any such order or give any such directions."

6.4. It should be observed that the costs rules only apply where there is either a change of title, *i.e.* where the proprietorship changes in some way or where an exclusive licence is granted. Where, for instance, a mortgage is granted so that the patent is subject to a charge in favour of the lender in case of default then failure to register the mortgage does not engage the adverse costs rules, though it should be borne in mind that failure to register transactions, even those not having costs consequences, can produce difficult effects since priorities are determined in order of registration so that, for instance, a first mortgagee may have to yield preference to a second mortgagee if the second mortgagee registered their mortgage first.

6.5. Why might assignments be relevant as between employees and employers? Given the description of the law given above, it is hoped that readers will appreciate that the path to employer ownership of employee inventions is far from straightforward. In some cases, employers will acknowledge that their right as against the employee is difficult or costly to assert and in some of those cases, employers and employees may well negotiate an assignment from employee to employer (though the employee retains the right to be mentioned as the inventor at all times pursuant to s.13). That negotiation is perfectly proper and the outcome of any negotiation is a matter for the free choices and leverage of the parties. The parties may agree a contract, a bare assignment or an assignment by deed. The last two of these require formalities; deeds (essentially documents having the effects of a contract but with consideration only passing one way) having to be signed and signature witnessed and assignments required to be in writing and signed by the assignor.

6.6. **Illustration**: An employee has agreed to assign his patent to his employer. He wants to do this in a contract. What are the words of conveyance effective under s.30? The parties consult a lawyer and the lawyer advises that the following wording will suffice to transfer the patent from employer to employee:-

> "The assignor assigns to the assignee all his right, title and interest in and to [patent m [number]] or [patent application m [number]] or [any patent or application for a patent deriving priority from patent application m [number]], including any inventions disclosed therein."

6.7. The employer should beware though, an employer has a right to apply for additional compensation in certain circumstances, no matter how generous any purchase agreement is (though the level is to be taken into account). This aspect is dealt with further below.

6.8. Section 42 declares that any term in a contract relating to inventions shall be unenforceable where that invention is made by an employee and where the contract is made with their employer or another at the request of the employer and which diminishes the rights of that employee in their inventions. This has led some to question whether the provision precludes an obligation on an employee to assign a patent of a future invention, however since assignments are specifically envisaged by s.40(2)(b) then it is questionable whether the expression 'employee invention' means any invention whatsoever. Rather, it means any invention falling within the ambit of employee inventions envisaged by s.39 (inventions arising in the course of duties where inventions may be expected to result) – see *KCI Licensing Inc* v. *Smith & Nephew Plc* [2010] EWHC 1487 (Pat), Arnold J.

CHAPTER SEVEN
ENTITLEMENT

7.1. Section 7(4) states that "except so far as the contrary is established, a person who makes an application for a patent shall be taken to be the person who is entitled under sub s(2) above to be granted a patent and two or more persons who make such an application jointly shall be taken to be the persons so entitled." Accordingly, although s.7(1) states that anybody may apply for a patent but s.7(4) leaves it open to establish the contrary. Where this takes place then then dispute process before a court or tribunal is called entitlement or entitlement proceedings.

7.2. The inventor is an individual '... who came up with the inventive concept. His contribution must be to the formulation of that concept' – *University of Southampton's Applications* [2005] RPC 11, H.L. If that person was an employee and the rules (engaged to invent and inventions might be expected to result) apply then the employer is entitled. However, what constituted the engagement might be very nuanced. If an employee is engaged to invent in one area and in fact ends up inventing in another then that will not do. Indeed this question was considered in *LIFFE v Pinkava* [2007] EWCA Civ 217, C.A.. In that case the employee (Pinkava) had been employed to devise certain novel products of a particular description. The employee, in fact, created other products which fell outside the description. Hence, so the employee argued, he was the inventor and the displacing provisions of s.39 did not apply, entitling him to the resultant patent. The judge at first instance accepted the contention of the employee, that what

he did fell outside his normal duties but went on to find as
fact that the employee had been specifically assigned the duty
to invent more widely, and therefore his employer was
entitled to the patent. On appeal by the employee the Court
of Appeal came to the view that the judge below was wrong
to find that what the employee did was outside his normal
duties since, on the facts, the employee's remit was very wide
and certainly wide enough to catch what he actually invented.
Accordingly, there was no need to examine the question of
specifically assigned duties.

7.3.   It is therefore important to keep clear records of what an
employee is asked to do within their normal or specific duties
to avoid uncertainty as to whether an invention was arrived at
in the course of those duties. It is all too common that
employment contracts start with a clear position on employee
duties but as years pass the terms of the contract may no
longer fully reflect the role of the employee. This change of
role and duties over time could be construed against the
employers' interest and so employers should regularly re-con-
sider the duties described in the terms of the contract, or
maintain employee files that show the revisions over time.

7.4.   If an employee suggests that their invention is not one made
within the course of their employment and normal duties,
then it is worth considering the requirement in s.39(1)(b)
that the employee might be under a 'special obligation' to
further his employer's undertaking. This was considered in
Harris' Patent [1985] R.P.C. 19, Falconer J. The judge found
that two conditions had to be satisfied, being (i) that the
invention was made in the course of the duties of the
employee; and (ii) that because of the nature of those duties
and the particular responsibilities arising from the nature of

those duties, a special obligation to further an employer's interests existed. With regard to condition (ii) Falconer J stated that much would depend on the facts of each case but that the more senior the person, a managing director for instance, the more likely it is that a special duty would exist.

What does the course of normal or specifically assigned duties mean?

7.5. There can be situations where an employee creates an invention and it is not immediately clear if this was done in the course of his duties as an employee. This may be because it is done in their own time, at their home, using their own equipment. In those situations, a factual review will be needed to determine whether the invention was in the course of their duties.

7.6. In *Alexander Ritchie v Envireneer Marine Cranes* – O/220/06, a decision of the Comptroller of Patents, Designs and Trade Marks is an example of how notwithstanding that an employee's primary role was not one where the duties might lead to an invention, the Employer might still be entitled. In that case, an engineering project manager, Ritchie, devised the invention; a lifting device for use in the offshore industry, while he was employed by Offshore Crane Engineering (OCE). In recognition that this was outside his normal duties OCE agreed to reward Ritchie by paying him a royalty on sales of the invention in return for an assignment of the patent to OCE. One would have thought from those acts that OCE was acknowledging that Ritchie was entitled. OCE subsequently went into liquidation and its assets were purchased by TSI (Crane) Limited (TSI). Mr Ritchie then claimed that as a result of an agreement he had with OCE, that upon OCE's insolvency the patent (or any application for a patent) would be transferred to him. However, despite the position of OCE recognising his inventiveness outside Ritchie's normal duties, it was found that he possessed knowledge of engineering such that it was reasonable to expect that he might invent something while carrying out his duties, and consequently he did arrive at his invention in the course of those duties. It is of importance to note that both the duty and expectation aspects must be satisfied. As it was found that although the duties were outside the course of his normal duties, they had been specifically assigned to him, and so the requirements were met. It was therefore held that the employer was entitled to apply for the patent; at that stage the application was still being considered by the Patent Office and no patent had actually been granted. Consequently, OCE as the employer was initially entitled to apply to patent the invention and as TSI purchased the business they were entitled to prosecute the application to patent the invention.

7.7. The Courts will not always find an invention is the property of the employer though, as the *Harris Patent* decision demonstrates. In that case the patent concerned a slide valve and was an improvement over a 'Wey' valve. Mr. Harris made the slide valve invention while he was manager of the Wey valve department of his employer. In August 1978 Harris was told that his function had become redundant and he left the company in December 1978; the slide valve invention was devised between those dates. He applied for the patent in January 1979, and his employer claimed to be entitled by reason of s. 39(1). Mr Harris' primary duty was to sell Wey valves and to deal with problems experienced by customers. The employer had no research laboratory, and never undertook any creative design activity; any major problem was referred to the Swedish parent company for a solution. Mr Harris' role did not involve any real management of the business, and the Comptroller of Patents, Designs and Trade Marks' hearing officer decided that the patent belonged to Mr Harris, as he was not employed to design or invent and did not have a special obligation to further his employer's interests.

7.8. On appeal to the Patents Court, the hearing officer's decision was upheld, the Court finding that:

- The circumstances in which the invention was made, rather than those in which any invention whatsoever might have been made, were the 'circumstances' referred to in s.39(1)(a).

- An employee's normal duties were the actual duties which he was employed to do. His duty of fidelity to his employer was to carry out faithfully his normal duties to the best of his ability and did not assist in formulating what those duties were.

- As the employer never took it upon themselves to solve design problems in the valves, it could not have been part of Harris' normal duties to provide solutions to such problems. The invention was not made in the course of Harris's normal duties, nor was it made in circumstances such that an invention might reasonably be expected to have resulted from his carrying out his normal duties.

- The extent and nature of an employee's obligation to further the interests of the employer's undertaking depended on the employee's status and the attendant duties and responsibilities of that status. Harris had only an obligation to effect sales of Wey valves and to ensure after-sales service to customers of valves supplied; accordingly his invention did not fall within s.39(1)(b).

7.9. The court therefore held that the expression 'an invention' in s.39(1)(a) cannot mean any invention whatsoever. It is governed by the qualification that it has to be an invention that might reasonably be expected to result from the carrying out of the duties of the employee. The expectation is that invention contributes to achieving an objective which is within the employee's duties (including those specifically assigned).

7.10. The position in *Harris' Patent* has been more recently considered by the court in in *LIFFE Administration and Management v Pavel Pinkava and De Novo Markets Limited* [2006] EWHC 595 (Pat), Kit6chin J. where he cautioned against using the *Harris Patent* case as a substitute for the statutory test in s39(1)(a). s39(1)(a), which required that an invention might reasonably be expected to result from the carrying out of the duties of an employee, was not to be satisfied if any invention actually resulted. It had to be specific to the duties in question.

7.11. When considering the normal duties of an employee, whilst the Court in *Harris' Patent* found that the employee had a duty to his employer to further its undertaking to the best of his ability; consideration of that duty did not *per se* assist in the formulation of the actual duties he is employed to do. However, this must be considered in light of the decision in *LIFFE*, where the Court of Appeal held that although the source of an employee's duty is primarily contractual, the contract evolves in the course of time such that it is unsafe to have regard only to the terms contained in an initial written contract of employment.

7.12. Where the invention does belong to an employee and the employee wishes to work the invention then he may need to do so (and may only be able to do so) by using their employer's other creations such as specifications, plans and drawings, where the intellectual property rights protecting those other creations is owned by the employer. s39(2) provides that if the employee wishes to pursue an application for a patent or wishes to perform or work the invention, then carrying out those acts will not amount to an infringement of any copyright or design right in any model or document relating to the invention. However, this is a trap for the unwary, since it does not enable the use of know-how or confidential information or the right to use technologies protected by other means of intellectual property right, such as registered design right, database right and other patents. If, for instance there are blocking or feeder technology patents then this may have the effect of rendering the employee's patent moribund.

Entitlement – the case to be put for judicial determination

7.13. Entitlement is dealt with in sections 8-13, 37 and 82 & 83, though sections 82 & 83 concern jurisdiction. Section 8 is concerned with deciding pre-grant entitlement issues and s9 is a transfer provision which deals with the position if a pre-grant entitlement action is gotten going but grant intervenes; in that case s.9 transfers the case to an application under s37, which concerns dealing with post grant situations. Section 10 is concerned with what is to be done where there are joint applicants and they get into a dispute about how to proceed with an application – it is not about whether a joint application should proceed in one name or another (that is the province of s.8). Section 11 deals with the consequences of a determination that an applicant (or in the cases dealt with under s.37 via s.9, the patentee or proprietor) is able to obtain an entitlement determination. Section 12 is equivalent to s8 but concerns foreign and convention patents (*i.e.* not just foreign patents but patents in prosecution in patent grant systems such as the EPO), but pre grant – if there is an intervening grant then the post-grant questions are to be dealt with under the national law of the patent and probably pursuant to the jurisdiction of the local entitlement tribunals. Section 12 applications are, in relation to EPO patents, subject to the jurisdiction provisions of sections 82 & 83. Section 13 is intended to deal with situations relating to inventorship disputes as to who should be properly mentioned as the inventor, though inventorship disputes can also give rise to applicant disputes as a knock-on effect.

7.14. A person claiming not to have been properly named as an inventor may apply to the Comptroller of Patents, Designs and Trade Marks for rectification of that position. The person claiming to be an inventor must be able to satisfy the comptroller that the applicant is the inventor or is the joint inventor. The inventor is the person who either alone or with others brought the inventive concept into being. The question is not to be looked at in the context of who contributed to which claim but rather to look at the person who did the thing in substance – *Henry Bros (Magherafelt) Ltd* v *Ministry of Defence (Revocation of Patent)* [1997] R.P.C. 693, Jacob J. That person may apply under s13 for a declaration accordingly or, as happened in *Henry Brothers* the defendant may defend a case against it on infringement on the basis that the patent was liable to be revoked because the claimant was not properly entitled as the inventor (and thus was not entitled to apply or proceed to grant) whereas, had it wished to apply, the defendant would be properly entitled as inventor (and thus was entitled to apply and to proceed to grant, even if it did not do so) – s72(1)(*b*).

7.15. Although a right to be mentioned as an inventor might at first glance seem anodyne, it may be far from so especially if the inventor is an employee, in which case they may be entitled to compensation or if the inventor thereby gains a right to be an applicant and thus a proprietor, in which case they gain a share of or all of any revenues arising from exploitation.

7.16. In other cases the issue might not be about an inventor at all – that might be a settled or uncontentious question, but, rather, the right to apply might be the issue. In those circumstances the person claiming to be an applicant or a joint applicant may apply under s8 for appropriate determination by the Comptroller. Here the issue is for the Comptroller to decide is whether the right to apply derives in an appropriate way. The jurisdiction to decide who is the appropriate applicant is derived from s.8 and thus applications under s8 may only be made before grant and orders made under s.8 may only be made before grant. If grant intervenes, *i.e.* the patent is granted, then s.9 decrees that the s8 application becomes a s.37 application instead. A s.7 application is an application to be declared the proprietor or some other lesser right of a proprietary nature (such as joint proprietorship). The Comptroller (or the court if he refers the matter to the court) may make an order adjusting the position. Importantly in accordance with s.37(5) the comptroller is not entitled to entertain any application made more than two years after grant unless it can be shown that the existing proprietor knew at the time of grant or transfer to him that he was not entitled.

7.17. Sometimes issues arise where foreign patent applications are the subject of contest as to who the proper proprietor is. The comptroller (or the court should he decide to refer the matter to the court) can decide the question. The jurisdiction of the comptroller is general, unless the or one of the foreign patent applications is an EPO patent (in which case s.82 applies – see below). The Comptroller also has jurisdiction to decide internecine disputes between joint applicants as he would under s.10 in relation to local patent applications. Where entitlement proceedings (whether in relation to foreign applications or local applications) are resolved in some way or other then the Comptroller has the power to direct that the applications proceed in some other manner by way of who the proper applicant is or who the proper applicants are (see s.12(1)). Any licences granted and any good faith working remains lawful (see sections 11 and 12(5)).

7.18. In some cases the comptroller under a reference under s13 (inventorship) and thence under s.8 (applicant entitled) may decide that the actual inventive concept was narrower than that to which the original patent related or in the case of joint applicants may decide that the inventors are in reality inventors of different concepts. In either case the Comptroller may under s.8(3) divide the antecedent applications out and bearing the old date of filing.

CHAPTER EIGHT
THE EMPLOYEE AS THE PROPRIETOR AND THE DUTY TO ACCOUNT

8.1. The aim of this short chapter is to deal with the reasoning of the court in the case of – *Ultraframe (UK) Limited* v. *Clayton* (m 2) and *Ultraframe UK Limited* v. *Fielding* (m 2) [2003] E.W.C.A. Civ 1805; [2004] E.C.D.R. 338; [2004] R.P.C. 479; (2004) 101(5) L.S.G. 29; *The Times*, January 12, 2004, C.A.

8.2. The *Ultraframe* rule (though the actual rule antedates the *Ultraframe* case) states simply that where one person (a servant) owes duties of fidelity to another (usually a master) then the servant is bound to account to the master for anything coming into his possession or his thoughts which result in a manifestation and which may benefit the master.

8.3. This definition is apt to capture employer-employee relations since in one sense the employer-employee relationship is one of master and servant. The answer to this is that the law recognises employee relations in a different way and not strictly as an agency question. However the agency question may still arise whether it be by way of implied agency or an express agency, directorships, partners in a firm and *quasi* partners, being the most common example of agency arising, and where it does then it is the duty of the agent to employ that which he derives by reason of the existence and functioning of the agency for the benefit of his master and not to use that derived substance unfairly against the master either during the currency of the agency or subsequently.

8.4. The accurate position was expressed by Waller L.J. In *Ultra-frame* in the following way (formatting and explanatory words added) at [2004] R.P.C. 407:-

> "39. Certain fundamental principles can I think be expressed in the following propositions.
>
> (1) It is the duty of any agent to employ the materials and information obtained by reason of his agency solely for the purposes of the agency; the agent will be liable to account to his principal for profits made by that agent.
>
> (2) Directors including *de facto* directors are fiduciary agents for the company, and they are trustees of the property of the company in their hands or under their control.
>
> (3) An agent will not be liable to account if he is acting with the fully informed assent of the principal.
>
> (4) Directors of a company can neither lawfully use their powers except for the benefit of the company nor act *ultra vires* the company.
>
> (5) All the shareholders may relieve a director from liability from any breach of that director's duty, provided only that the breach is not *ultra vires* the company and does not involve a fraud on its creditors (see Gore-Brown , 44th ed., ¶ 27.21.2).
>
> (6) It would be *ultra vires* the company to distribute assets of a company to the shareholders other than:
>
> (*a*) by way of a distribution of profit lawfully made or

(*b*) by a reduction in capital duly sanctioned by the court or

(*c*) (possibly) a return of capital by the adoption of a special procedure under the Companies Acts. (see *Aveling Barford Limited* v *Perion Limited* [1989] B.C.L.C. 626 at 631, Hoffmann J.)."

CHAPTER NINE
THE EMPLOYER AS THE PROPRIETOR AND THE OBLIGATION TO COMPENSATE

9.1. Sections 39-43 deal with employee inventions by way of setting out the rules concerning the employer override (s.39) and employee compensation (sections 40-43). This chapter is concerned with employee compensation. The starting point is s.40 (showing amendment history):-

Compensation of employees for certain inventions

40.(1) Where it appears to the court or the comptroller on an application made by an employee within the prescribed period that

(a) the employee has made an invention belonging to the employer for which a patent has been granted, ~~that the patent is (~~

(b) having regard among other things to the size and nature of the employer's undertaking~~)~~, the invention or the patent for it (or the combination of both) is of outstanding benefit to the employer, and ~~that~~

(c) by reason of those facts it is just that the employee should be awarded compensation to be paid by the employer, the court or the comptroller may award him such compensation of an amount determined under s41 below.

(2) Where it appears to the court or the comptroller on an application made by an employee within the prescribed period that—

(a) a patent has been granted for an invention made by and belonging to the employee;

(b) his rights in the invention, or in any patent or application for a patent for the invention, have since the appointed day been assigned to the employer or an exclusive licence under the patent or application has since the appointed day been granted to the employer;

(c) the benefit derived by the employee from the contract of assignment, assignation or grant or any ancillary contract ("the relevant contract") is inadequate in relation to the benefit derived by the employer from the invention or the patent for it (or both); and

(d) by reason of those facts it is just that the employee should be awarded compensation to be paid by the employer in addition to the benefit derived from the relevant contract;

the court or the comptroller may award him such compensation of an amount determined under s41 below.

(3) Subsections (1) and (2) above shall not apply to the invention of an employee where a relevant collective agreement provides for the payment of compensation in respect of inventions of the same description as that

invention to employees of the same description as that employee.

(4) Subsection (2) above shall have effect notwithstanding anything in the relevant contract or any agreement applicable to the invention (other than any such collective agreement).

(5) If it appears to the comptroller on an application under this section that the application involves matters which would more properly be determined by the court, he may decline to deal with it.

(6) In this section—

"the prescribed period ", in relation to proceedings before the court, means the period prescribed by rules of court, and

"relevant collective agreement " means a collective agreement within the meaning of the Trade Union and Labour Relations (Consolidation) Act 1992[1974 c. 52.] Trade Union and Labour Relations Act 1974, made by or on behalf of a trade union to which the employee belongs, and by the employer or an employers' association to which the employer belongs which is in force at the time of the making of the invention.

(7) References in this to an invention belonging to an employer or employee are references to it so belonging as between the employer and the employee.

The amendments in sub s(1) and in paragraph (2)(c) were introduced with effect from the 1ˢᵗ of January 2005 by the

Patents Act 2004 and only relates to patents applied form after 1st of January 2005. The amendments in sub s(6) were introduced with effect from the 16th of October 1992 by the Trade Union and Labour Relations (Consolidation) Act 1992.

9.2.   The expression 'prescribed period' is defined in the Civil Procedure Rules (rule 63.12) as being the period from grant to one year after the patent ceases to have effect. If the expiry of the patent arose as a result of non-payment of renewal fees (referred to as default) then the patent is deemed to remain effective for the full term provided that renewal fees which could be paid late are paid. In some cases of bad default where the patent cases to be in a renewal limbo and ceases to have effect it may be necessary to apply for restoration of the patent (though the way in which this is done and the things which need to be proved are outside the scope of this chapter). If restoration is refused then the prescribed period expires 1 year from the date after the patent ceases to have effect or 6 months after the date of refusal whichever is the latter. Further the 'appointed day' appearing in sub s.(2) is the 1st of June 1978 (art 2 of the Patents Act 1977 (Commencement m 2) Order 1978 (S.I. 1978 m 586 (C.14))).

9.3.   As can be seen s.40 is divided into two parts which correspond with the situation where the employer gets the right to make a patent application because the employee is the correct kind of employee or the invention was derived in the correct way, *i.e.* properly on the employee's behalf – that is sub s(1), and then the situation where the employer derives the application or the patent by way of an assignment from the employee or where an exclusive licence is granted to the employer by the employee, in sub s.(2). These distinctions will be explored further below.

9.4. There is a quirky aspect to s.40, which is sub s.(7). There is it stated that s.40 is only concerned with situations where the employer has a <u>better</u> claim to be the applicant (and, for the first and last time, patentee or proprietor) than employee (and no other) and not with whether anybody has a better claim than the employer to be the applicant. In other words the effect of sub s(7) is to ensure that the employee cannot impugn the rights of the employer under s.39 by stating that a third party has a better claim to be an applicant than does the employer, though if the employee is claiming employee compensation it is unclear why he would want to do that. The employer and the third party can battle that issue out separately. However the operation of sub s(7) also operates in the converse; the employer cannot claim, in the context of a compensation claim by an employee, that it is not the properly entitled applicant (and therefore need not pay compensation) because somebody else has a better claim to that rôle. In other words, and to put somewhat colloquially, it precludes the employer from contending that somebody else owns the patent even if the employer-employee rules in s.39 apply so that compensation is not payable.

S.40(1) & (2) – patent, invention or both?

9.5. Under sub s(1) the court (which, for these purposes only, includes the Comptroller of Patents, Designs and Trade Marks) may award compensation to the employee if the application of compensation is made in time, that the invention or the patent for it or both are of outstanding benefit and that it is just that compensation be awarded –

that the patent or invention of outstanding benefit. Prior to 2005 it was the patent and only the patent which had to be of outstanding benefit. This was explained in *Memco-Med Ltd's Patent* [1992] RPC 403, 414, Aldous J. In *Memco* the technology concerned an improved unit for preventing lift doors from closing on a person getting into or out of a lift. Whilst there had been substantial sales of units incorporating the patented technology the patent itself was not of benefit, let alone outstanding benefit because all Memco's sales were made to a single customer, Otis. On one view Aldous J. found on the facts that the relationship between Memco and its single customer was unaffected by the patent – hence the patent was not of any, let alone any outstanding, benefit to Memco. The words used by Aldous J, are not apt to precise understanding; he said:-

> "Even if it be right that the … model [incorporating the patented technology] was of outstanding benefit to Memco-Med it does not follow that the patent has been of any benefit to Memco-Med. Its sales to Otis might have been just the same if the patent had never been granted."

9.6.   As one case see the word 'might' is mighty. To be fair to the judge though, what he was saying was that there was no evidence that the outstanding benefit came from the patent (as opposed to being from the invention) and that whilst evidence of sales volume might have been of some evidential value, those sales might also or equally have resulted from the price & quality of the product and the relationship with the client's buyer. The position could have been different if evidence was led from Otis to say that the patent was important to it but since there was no evidence of that kind the judge refused to make that inference.

9.7.   It was the *Memco* case and similar cases in the same vein which led to the amendment of sub s.(1) so that the focus of the court's enquiry included consideration of the benefit of the patent or the invention or both. As one can see had this been the test in 1992 when *Memco* was decided then the case could have been decided differently, since there was a greater scope for saying that the relationship between Memco and its single customer whilst unaffected by the patent was certainly positively affected by the innovation.

Section 41 – the mechanics

9.8.   Section 41 sets out what it is that the awarding tribunal must have regard to s.41 states, in all its glory, with amendments and so on, as follows:-

Amount of compensation.

41. (1) An award of compensation to an employee under s40(1) or (2) above ~~in relation to a patent for an invention~~ shall be such as will secure for the employee a fair share (having regard to all the circumstances) of the benefit which the employer has derived, or may reasonably be expected to derive, from any of the following

(a) the invention in question;

(b) the patent for the invention;

(c) ~~or from~~ the assignment, assignation or grant of-to a ~~person connected with the employer~~

(i) the property or any right in the invention, or

(ii) the property in, or any right in or under, an application for that patent

to a person connected with the employer.

(2) For the purposes of subs(1) above the amount of any benefit derived or expected to be derived by an employer from the assignment, assignation or grant of—

(a) the property in, or any right in or under, a patent for the invention or an application for such a patent; or

(b) the property or any right in the invention;

to a person connected with him shall be taken to be the amount which could reasonably be expected to be so derived by the employer if that person had not been connected with him.

(3) Where the Crown, United Kingdom Research and Innovation or a Research Council in its capacity as employer assigns or grants the property in, or any right in or under, an invention, patent or application for a patent to a body having among its functions that of developing or exploiting inventions resulting from public research and does so for no consideration or only a nominal consideration, any benefit derived from the invention, patent or application by that body shall be treated for the purposes of the foregoing provisions of this sas so derived by the Crown, United Kingdom Research and Innovation or the Research Council (as the case may be). In this subs "Research Council" means a body which is a Research Council for the purposes of the Science and Technology

Act 1965 ~~or the Arts and Humanities Research Council (as defined by s1 of the Higher Education Act 2004)~~.

(4) In determining the fair share of the benefit to be secured for an employee in respect of ~~a patent for~~ an invention which has always belonged to an employer, the court or the comptroller shall, among other things, take the following matters into account, that is to say—

(a) the nature of the employee's duties, his remuneration and the other advantages he derives or has derived from his employment or has derived in relation to the invention under this Act;

(b) the effort and skill which the employee has devoted to making the invention;

(c) the effort and skill which any other person has devoted to making the invention jointly with the employee concerned, and the advice and other assistance contributed by any other employee who is not a joint inventor of the invention; and

(d) the contribution made by the employer to the making, developing and working of the invention by the provision of advice, facilities and other assistance, by the provision of opportunities and by his managerial and commercial skill and activities.

(5) In determining the fair share of the benefit to be secured for an employee in respect of ~~a patent for~~ an invention which originally belonged to him, the court or the comptroller shall, among other things, take the following matters into account, that is to say—

(a) any conditions in a licence or licences granted under this Act or otherwise in respect of the invention or the patent for it;

(b) the extent to which the invention was made jointly by the employee with any other person; and

(c) the contribution made by the employer to the making, developing and working of the invention as mentioned in subs(4)(d) above.

(6) Any order for the payment of compensation under s40 above may be an order for the payment of a lump sum or for periodical payment, or both.

(7) Without prejudice to s~~32~~12 or s14 of the Interpretation Act ~~1889~~1978 c. 30, the refusal of the court or the comptroller to make any such order on an application made by an employee under s40 above shall not prevent a further application being made under that by him or any successor in title of his.

(8) Where the court or the comptroller has made any such order, the court or he may on the application of either the employer or the employee vary or discharge it or suspend any provision of the order and revive any provision so suspended, and s40(5) above shall apply to the application as it applies to an application under that section.

(9) In England and Wales any sums awarded by the comptroller under s40 above shall, if ~~a~~the county court so orders, be recoverable under s85 of the County Courts Act 1984 ~~by execution issued form the county court~~ or otherwise as if they were payable under an order of that court.

(10) In Scotland an order made under s40 above by the comptroller for the payment of any sums may be enforced in like manner as <u>an extract registered decree arbitral bearing a warrant for execution issued by the sheriff court of any sheriffdom in Scotland</u>.

(11) In Northern Ireland an order made under s40 above by the comptroller for the payment of any sums may be enforced as if it were a money judgment.

<u>(12) In the Isle of Man an order made under s40 above by the comptroller for the payment of any sums may be enforced as if it were a judgment or order of the court for the payment of money</u> ~~in like manner an execution issued out of the court.~~

9.9. The amendments to sub-s(1) were introduced, with associated deletions, by the Patents Act 2004 c. 16 s.10(3) (for patents applied for on or after 1st January 1, 2005. The words in sub-s3) were inserted by the Higher Education and Research Act 2017 c. 29 sch 12 para 13(a) (from 1st April 2018). The words in sub s(3) were inserted by the Higher Education and Research Act 2017 c. 29 sch 12 para 13(b) (from 1st of April 2018), though the substituted, then subsequently stricken words were originally inserted by the Higher Education Act 2004 c. 8 sch 6 para 5 (from 16th December 2004 and then repealed by the Higher Education and Research Act 2017 c. 29 sch 12 para 13(c) (from 1st of April 2018). The words in sub ss(4) and (5) were repealed by the Patents Act 2004 c. 16 s10(4) & 10(5) respectively (in relation to patents applied for on or after 1st January 2005). The words in sub s(7) were substituted by virtue of the Interpretation Act 1978 (c. 30), s25(2). The words 'the county court' in sub-s(9) were substituted by the Crime and Courts

Act 2013 c. 22 sch 9(3) para 52(1)(b) (April 22, 2014: substitution has effect as SI 2014/954 subject to savings and transitional provisions specified in 2013 c.22 s15 and sch 8 and transitional provision specified in SI 2014/954 arts 2(c) and 3). The remaining words in sub s(9) were substituted by the Tribunals, Courts and Enforcement Act 2007 c. 15 sch 13 para 40 (from 6th of April 2014). The words in sub s(10) were substituted by the Patents Act 2004 c. 16 sch 2 para 11 (from 1st of January 2004). Finally sub s12 was added by The Patents Act 1977 (Isle of Man) Order 1978 (SI 1978 m 621), replaced by The Patents Act 1977 (Isle of Man) Order 2003 (SI 2003 m 1249) and amended by The Patents Act 1977 (Isle of Man) Order 2013 (SI 2013 m 2602).

9.10. To some extent the provisions of s.41 (sub ss(3) and (6)-(11)) are self explanatory or relate to circumstances which are too specialised to come within the scope of this text. Sub s(1) instructs the court to remember that the benefit is to be measured by reference to the benefit provided by the patent or the invention (for the purposes of s40(1) – employer owned inventions or patents) or for the benefit provided by the exploitation patent or the invention (for the purposes of s.40(2) – employee owned inventions or patents but subsequently assigned or licenced). Sub s(2) on the other hands instructs the court to consider benefit in assignment or licencing cases envisaged by s.40(2) by reference to notional assignment or licencing negotiations on an arms length.

9.11. Sub-section (4) concerns the exercise carried out in s.40(1) – employer owned inventions. Sub-section (5) on the other hand concerns the exercise carried out in s.40(2) – employee owned inventions.

Sections 41(4) and 40(1) – employer owned inventions and fair share of benefit

9.12. Section 41(4) (and thus s.40(1)) requires the tribunal to have regard to the nature of the employee's duties and the remuneration package (whether derived from employment or from the invention), her skill or effort and that of any other and the infrastructure and other assistance (including advice, the provision of opportunities and managerial & commercial skill) provided by the employer. These things are difficult to measure and ultimately concern facts which are unlikely to have been recorded by those concerned at the relevant time. It is in this regard that policies are helpful in protecting or at least crystallising the position of both parties, though it is to be borne in mind that there can be a drastic difference between policies and practice.

9.13. It is to be observed that it might be unclear whether the additional assistance by others (defined as effort and skill) should be inventive. The very wording implies not as it would be just as easy for the draughtsman of s.41(4)(*b*) & (*c*) to use the words "inventive contribution", hence mere facilitation will do. This is an unsurprising conclusion since an inventive contribution to the inventive concept would enable joint inventorship which takes the issue of contribution and benefit into a different realm unrelated to employee invention issues.

Section 41(5) and 40(2) – employee owned inventions which are exploited and fair share of benefit

9.14. The position concerning benevolent employees is different. It is how well the employer has done with the invention in terms of its exploitation whether by way of assignment or by way of a licence which ultimately matters, though the contributions of others, if inventive, is to be taken into account, as well as the employer's contribution overall which goes into the mix when it comes to taking matters into account for the purposes of measuring benefit. It is clearer in s41(5) that the employer's contribution need not be inventive but that anything which eases the way is to be taken into account. The question is, however, how? If the invention would not have been derived but for the contribution of the employer then that is likely to be a serious factor in favouring an award which favours the employer. If, on the other hand, all that was involved was thought experiments then the show plays the other way.

Section 40(1) – outstanding benefit having regard to the size and nature of the employer's undertaking.

9.15. The word 'outstanding' has been the subject of a great deal of consideration over the years. In *Kelly and Chiu* v. *GE Healthcare Ltd* [2009] E.W.H.C. 181; [2009] R.P.C. 12, Floyd J. a review of all of the pre-existing authorities was carried out; the position was summarised by the judge in the following way:-

> '"Outstanding" means "something special" or "out of the ordinary" and more than "substantial", "significant" or "good". The benefit must be something more than one would normally expect to arise from the duties for which the employee is paid.'

9.16. *Kelly and Chiu* was cited with approval by the Supreme Court in *Ian Alexander Shanks* v. (1) *Unilever Plc*, (2) *Unilever*

Naamloze Vennootschap and (3) *Unilever UK Central Resources Limited* [2019] U.K.S.C. 45; [2019] 1 W.L.R. 5997; [2020] 2 All E.R. 733; [2019] Bus. L.R. 2730; *The Times*, November 19, 2019, S.C. overturning [2017] E.W.C.A. 2; [2017] Bus. L.R. 883; [2017] R.P.C. 522, C.A. affirming [2014] E.W.H.C. 1647; [2014] R.P.C. 829; (2014) 158(23) S.J.L.B. 41, Arnold J. affirming O/259/13, Comptroller of Patents, Designs and Trade Marks, though it may be observed that construing words by reference to what they do not mean and construing them by reference to other words is simply replacing one problem with another, which is hardly helpful.

9.17. In *Shanks* the Supreme Court was faced with a particular factual problem. The employee worked for a company called CRL, which was owned by Unilever Plc. CRL was to all intents and purposes a CRO providing research content to other companies in a group owned by Unilever Plc and a sister company Unilever NV. Hence CRL was a member of a large multifaceted corporate structure, which had the group name, Unilever. CRL was the relevant employer. CRL assigned all it could assign in relation to the employee's invention (for £100) to Unilever Plc, who retained the rights for the UK, Australia and Canada but thence assigned the rights for elsewhere in Europe, Japan and the USA to U NV (for £100). Unilever NV later assigned the rights for the USA to another company in the group called UPH BV. Both Unilever Plc and Unilever NV filed patent applications with various authorities. The net return of the patented technology was something of the order of £24m (which was deigned to be a benefit because of a connected companies stipulation at s.41(2), so that the value to be attributed was the open market value), even though the return to CRL was next to zero. The question was how the employer's undertaking was defined. If it was the group then £24m could be regarded as a mere pittance (since this was a very wealthy organisation overall) whereas if it was CRL then £24m might represent a great deal and so might amount to an outstanding benefit. However this was not without difficulty since if the £24m was to be attributed to CRL then so must the value of all the other patents which ultimately came from CRL be equally attributed, making CRL a rich man of straw. Either way the employee was faced with a difficulty which is that no matter how you attributed the £24m the benefit could not be described as outstanding. The difficulty with the group wide approach was that you would be comparing benefit derived from patents to, say, benefits obtained through skilled buying strategies – this did not seem apt to their lordships.

9.18. The Supreme Court looked at this later question, through which binoculars does one use to define the size and nature of the employer's undertaking(?), and answered this question with words equivalent to 'it depends,' as indeed it does since it is a factual enquiry and depends upon the size and nature of the employer's undertaking – note 'size' and 'nature.' It is a fact sensitive enquiry which involves looking at all the detail of the operation of the parent concern. Importantly a large organisation is likely to be of a multifaceted nature where a great many contributions are made to the income stream. The Supreme Court stated that in making the factual enquiry, it would be unfair to compare or rank all these income streams with one another. In the instant case, notwithstanding that the sum of £24m was dwarfed by the turnover and profits of Unilever as a whole, the Unilever group as a whole made a wide range of products which generated billions in sales and hundreds of millions in profits over the life of the patents which relate to that range. Key to the reasoning of the Supreme Court was that the rate of return on many of those 'other' patents was much lower than on the patents in issue. The Supreme Court's reasoning (expressed by Lord Kitchen JSC, an erstwhile Patents Court judge and a highly experienced patent lawyer in practice before then) was crystallised in the following way (formatting added):-

> "51. ... Many different aspects of the size and nature of the employer's business may be relevant to the enquiry. For example the benefit ...
>
> • may be more than would normally have been expected to arise from the duties for which the employee was paid,
>
> • it may have been arrived at without any risk to the business,
>
> • it may represent an extraordinarily high rate of return or
>
> • it may have been the opportunity to develop a new line of business or to engage in unforeseen licensing opportunities.
>
> In the circumstances of this case and for the reasons I have given, a highly material consideration must be the extent of the benefit of the Shanks patents to the Unilever group and how that compares with the benefits the group derived from other patents resulting from the work carried out at CRL."

9.19. The Supreme Court also went on to consider other matters, which were of importance in conducting the enquiry. Specifically the compensation was classed as a business expense, which would be taxable in the employee's hands. Additionally it appears to be accepted that account should properly be taken of the change in the value of money from the time of receipt of the relevant income by the employer to its payment to the employee.

9.20. On the question of outstanding benefit, the Supreme Court stated that whilst the connected undertakings rule applied the relevant organisation to consider was CRL and that the correct approach was to look at the value of the various patents which the Unilever group had – the patent in the instant case stood out, *i.e.* was outstanding. The Supreme Court further found that the Unilever group's size did not lend any additional weight to the success of the patens in issue and finally ruled that it was important to compare like with like. Looked at in that way compensation ought to be awarded.

9.21. It should be said that the approach of the court when looking at the size and nature of smaller organisations, such as a one patent firm or a single activity firm would be different but, in truth, that is because many of the features which Lord Kitchin identified in *Shanks* were never there in the first place.

9.22. The final piece of the jigsaw was to ascertain what constituted a fair share. In this respect the Supreme Court considered that 5% was a fair share and that the reasoning of the original tribunal could not be faulted. The issue of what proportion to award is a bit hit and miss and indeed there is nowhere in any of the multitude of reported *Shanks* cases any analysis of the economics of what is fair. Construed literally the word "fair" tends to mean equality of arms, so that an employee negotiating with an employer must be taken to negotiate in equal terms so that (as follows) things like might, demand and so on should not matter. Rather the tribunals in *Shanks* debated the employee rate of return on the basis of comparators in negotiated settlements (where, unfortunately, the content of those negotiations was never analysed). The furthest that the tribunals went was to say that a lower award was warranted where the employer had either put resources at risk or, by reason if its negotiating might, had, in actual licencing negotiations, managed to negotiate higher licence payments. In this latter respect it is difficult to see that "mere might" is conclusive one way or another. The leverage in question may arise for a variety of reasons, including the isolated originality of the invention, negotiating skill, market demand, the extent of the patent cliffs which both licensee and licensor are sitting on and the resources of the licensor to itself exploit. In other words there is no set formula. Furthermore where fairness has been discussed as between employer and employee it is unclear whether this fairness translates to considering potential licencing negotiations between employer and a potential or actual licensee. On the one hand it should since otherwise how does one compensate for inept licensors and on the other it should not since what matters is the benefit to the employer howsoever achieved, whether consequent on ineptitude or not. As Lord Kitchen would undoubtedly say (and as your authors humbly submit he might say – though he did not) – at some stage there has to be a figure and there has to be an end to it.

Section 40(2) – the benefit derived by the employee from the various contractual and like arrangements is inadequate in relation to the benefit derived by the employer.

9.23. In s. 40(1) the enquiry is directed to the outstanding benefit having regard to the size and nature of the employer's undertaking. Those words are very different from the stipulation in s40(2) – the question moves from the just reward arising from outstanding benefit derived by the employer from contribution to the adequacy of the employee's comparative benefit derived from exploitation, though it would be wholly wrong to say that exploitation benefits are not relevant in relation to employer owned inventions. Thus if the employee invents and the rights in (*i.e.* the property in) or under (*i.e.* forms of permission to use) that invention are transmitted to the employer by means of a contract between employer and employee, whether a contract of assignment or a licencing agreement (termed "the relevant contract") then the reward – if it is just to provide that reward – to the employee is additional to the consideration passing by means of the relevant contract.

9.24. The relevant contract includes, in addition to an assignment contract or a licencing contract, an ancillary contract, *i.e.* a contract which provides necessary support – and the support must be necessary in some way – to the notion of transfer of ownership or to the notion of licencing rights. The notion of how an ancillary contract might arise is irrelevant; what is important is that there is a contract which relates to the invention in some way and that consideration passes to the employee. In those circumstances it is the adequacy of that consideration which is important when the tribunal decides whether to make additional awards to the employee. The courts have yet to test the law set out in s.40(2).

S41 – the amount of compensation.

9.25. The function of the tribunal is evidence based on establishing the benefit actually achieved. However, the tribunal may speculate as to future earnings since that is the intention behind the words "may reasonably be expected to derive".

Section 41(2) – connected persons

9.26. Section 41(2) provides that is there is an internal assignment or licence between entities which are connected in an attempt to evade the benefit rules then the consideration for the assignment or licence shall be made on the basis that the transactions took place on an arms length basis. Connections are to be measured in the same way that connectivity works in tax situations, via s839 of the Income and Corporation Taxes Act 1988. In summary it includes families, partnerships and in corporate cases common ownership lineal control. However the only thing which matters is the connection between assigning or licencing parties. Their characteristics, bargaining power and leverage were to be taken in to account, their connection was not – *Ian Alexander Shanks* v. (1) *Unilever Plc*, (2) *Unilever Naamloze Vennootschap* and (3) *Unilever UK Central Resources Limited* [2010] E.W.C.A. 1283; [2011] R.P.C. 352, C.A.1

MORE BOOKS BY
LAW BRIEF PUBLISHING

A selection of our other titles available now:-

'Covid-19, Homeworking and the Law – The Essential Guide to Employment and GDPR Issues' by Forbes Solicitors
'Covid-19, Force Majeure and Frustration of Contracts – The Essential Guide' by Keith Markham
'Covid-19 and Criminal Law – The Essential Guide' by Ramya Nagesh
'Covid-19 and Family Law in England and Wales – The Essential Guide' by Safda Mahmood
'Covid-19 and the Implications for Planning Law – The Essential Guide' by Bob Mc Geady & Meyric Lewis
'Covid-19, Residential Property, Equity Release and Enfranchisement – The Essential Guide' by Paul Sams and Louise Uphill
'Covid-19, Brexit and the Law of Commercial Leases – The Essential Guide' by Mark Shelton
'Covid-19 and the Law Relating to Food in the UK and Republic of Ireland – The Essential Guide' by Ian Thomas
'A Practical Guide to the General Data Protection Regulation (GDPR) – 2nd Edition' by Keith Markham
'Ellis on Credit Hire – Sixth Edition' by Aidan Ellis & Tim Kevan
'A Practical Guide to Working with Litigants in Person and McKenzie Friends in Family Cases' by Stuart Barlow
'Protecting Unregistered Brands: A Practical Guide to the Law of Passing Off' by Lorna Brazell
'A Practical Guide to Secondary Liability and Joint Enterprise Post-Jogee' by Joanne Cecil & James Mehigan

'A Practical Guide to Financial Services Claims' by Chris Hegarty

'The Law of Houses in Multiple Occupation: A Practical Guide to HMO Proceedings' by Julian Hunt

'A Practical Guide to Unlawful Eviction and Harassment' by Stephanie Lovegrove

'A Practical Guide to Solicitor and Client Costs' by Robin Dunne

'Occupiers, Highways and Defective Premises Claims: A Practical Guide Post-Jackson – 2nd Edition' by Andrew Mckie

'A Practical Guide to Financial Ombudsman Service Claims' by Adam Temple & Robert Scrivenor

'A Practical Guide to Advising Schools on Employment Law' by Jonathan Holden

'A Practical Guide to Running Housing Disrepair and Cavity Wall Claims: 2nd Edition' by Andrew Mckie & Ian Skeate

'A Practical Guide to Holiday Sickness Claims – 2nd Edition' by Andrew Mckie & Ian Skeate

'Arguments and Tactics for Personal Injury and Clinical Negligence Claims' by Dorian Williams

'A Practical Guide to QOCS and Fundamental Dishonesty' by James Bentley

'A Practical Guide to Drone Law' by Rufus Ballaster, Andrew Firman, Eleanor Clot

'A Practical Guide to Compliance for Personal Injury Firms Working With Claims Management Companies' by Paul Bennett

'A Practical Guide to the Landlord and Tenant Act 1954: Commercial Tenancies' by Richard Hayes & David Sawtell

'A Practical Guide to Dog Law for Owners and Others' by Andrea Pitt

'RTA Allegations of Fraud in a Post-Jackson Era: The Handbook – 2nd Edition' by Andrew Mckie

'RTA Personal Injury Claims: A Practical Guide Post-Jackson' by Andrew Mckie

'On Experts: CPR35 for Lawyers and Experts' by David Boyle

'An Introduction to Personal Injury Law' by David Boyle

'A Practical Guide to Chronic Pain Claims' by Pankaj Madan
'A Practical Guide to Claims Arising from Fatal Accidents' by James Patience
'A Practical Guide to Subtle Brain Injury Claims' by Pankaj Madan

These books and more are available to order online direct from the publisher at www.lawbriefpublishing.com, where you can also read free sample chapters. For any queries, contact us on 0844 587 2383 or mail@lawbriefpublishing.com.

Our books are also usually in stock at www.amazon.co.uk with free next day delivery for Prime members, and at good legal bookshops such as Wildy & Sons.

We are regularly launching new books in our series of practical day-to-day practitioners' guides. Visit our website and join our free newsletter to be kept informed and to receive special offers, free chapters, etc.

You can also follow us on Twitter at www.twitter.com/lawbriefpub.